D0246795

This book belongs to:

Seaside

ALAIN GRÉE

Seaside

First published 2013 by Button Books, an imprint of Guild of Master Craftsman Publications Ltd, Castle Place, 166 High Street, Lewes, East Sussex BN7 1XU. Text © GMC Publications Ltd, 2013. Copyright in the Work © GMC Publications Ltd, 2013 Illustrations © 2013 A.G. & RicoBel. ISBN 978 1 90898 510 1.

A catalogue record for this book is available from the British Library.
Publisher: Jonathan Bailey; Production Manager: Jim Bulley; Managing Editor: Gerrie Purcell; Senior Project Editors: Sara Harper, Cath Senker; Managing Art Editor: Gilda Pacitti; Colour origination by GMC Reprographics; Printed and bound in China.

We're going to the seaside!

Our friends who live at the seaside have sent us some postcards. We're going to visit them for a holiday!

We wonder what it will be like at the seaside.
What will we see and do when we're there?

What shall we take?

What shall we pack in our suitcases to take on holiday to the seaside?

suitcases

clothes and shoes

hairbrush and comb

bucket and spade

beach ball

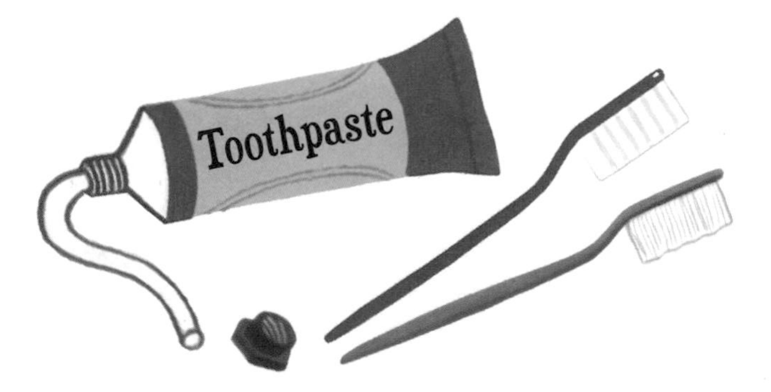

toothpaste and toothbrushes

colouring pencils and
a colouring book

camera

sunhat

sunglasses

suncream

umbrella

Let's put the last things
in our suitcases – then
we're ready to go!

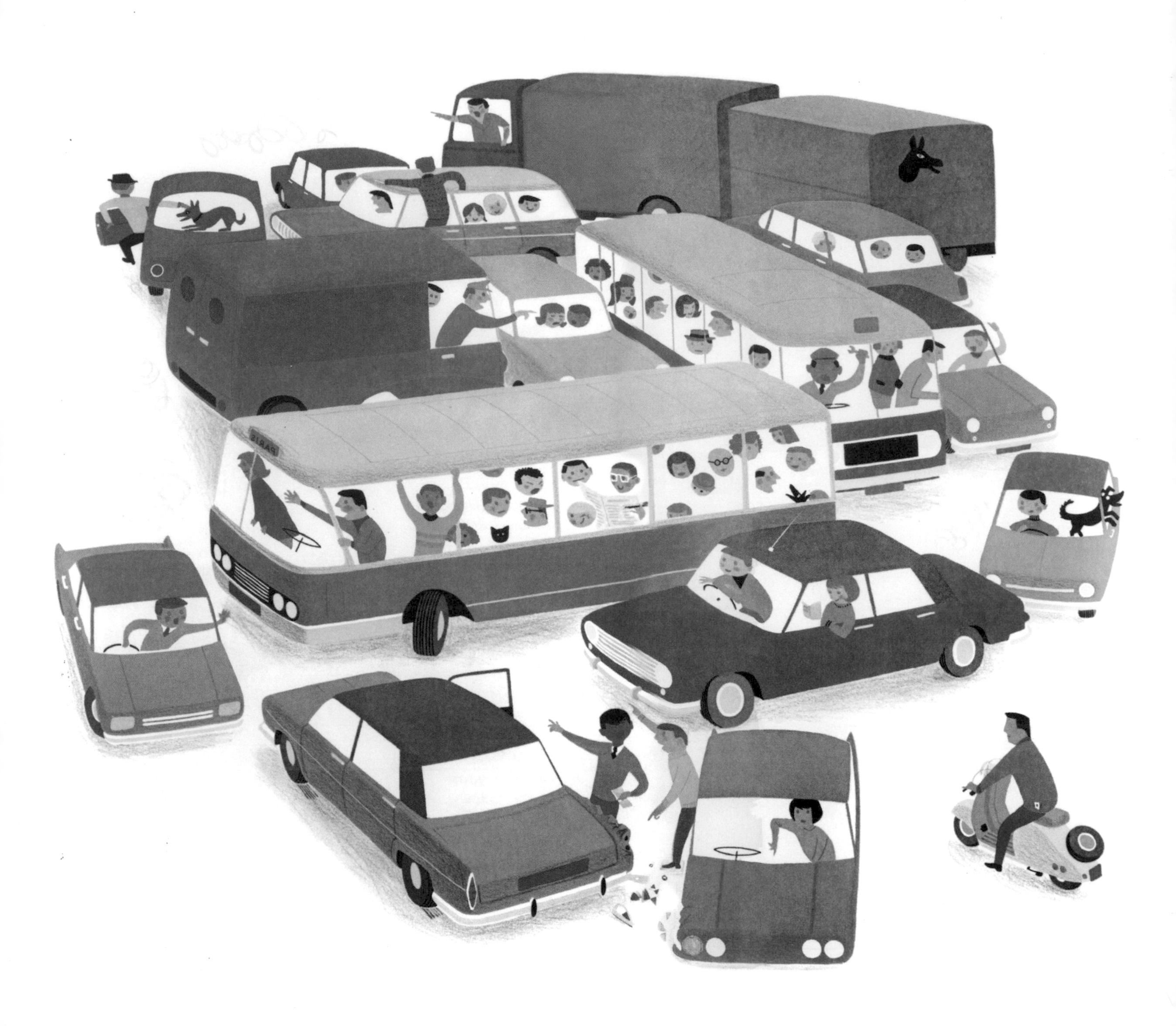

How shall we travel to the seaside? We could go by car. But it's the summer holidays, and lots of people are going to the seaside. Look at the traffic! Let's go by train instead.

We go to the railway station to buy our tickets.

Our train leaves in just ten minutes, so let's hurry to the platform. If we're quick, we'll find seats by the window!

ticket seller

train tickets

We're on board and our train is ready. Off we go to the seaside.

We're going to stay with our friends in their house at the seaside. Some people stay in a caravan or a tent at a campsite when they go on holiday. Others stay in hotels and guesthouses. Where would you like to stay?

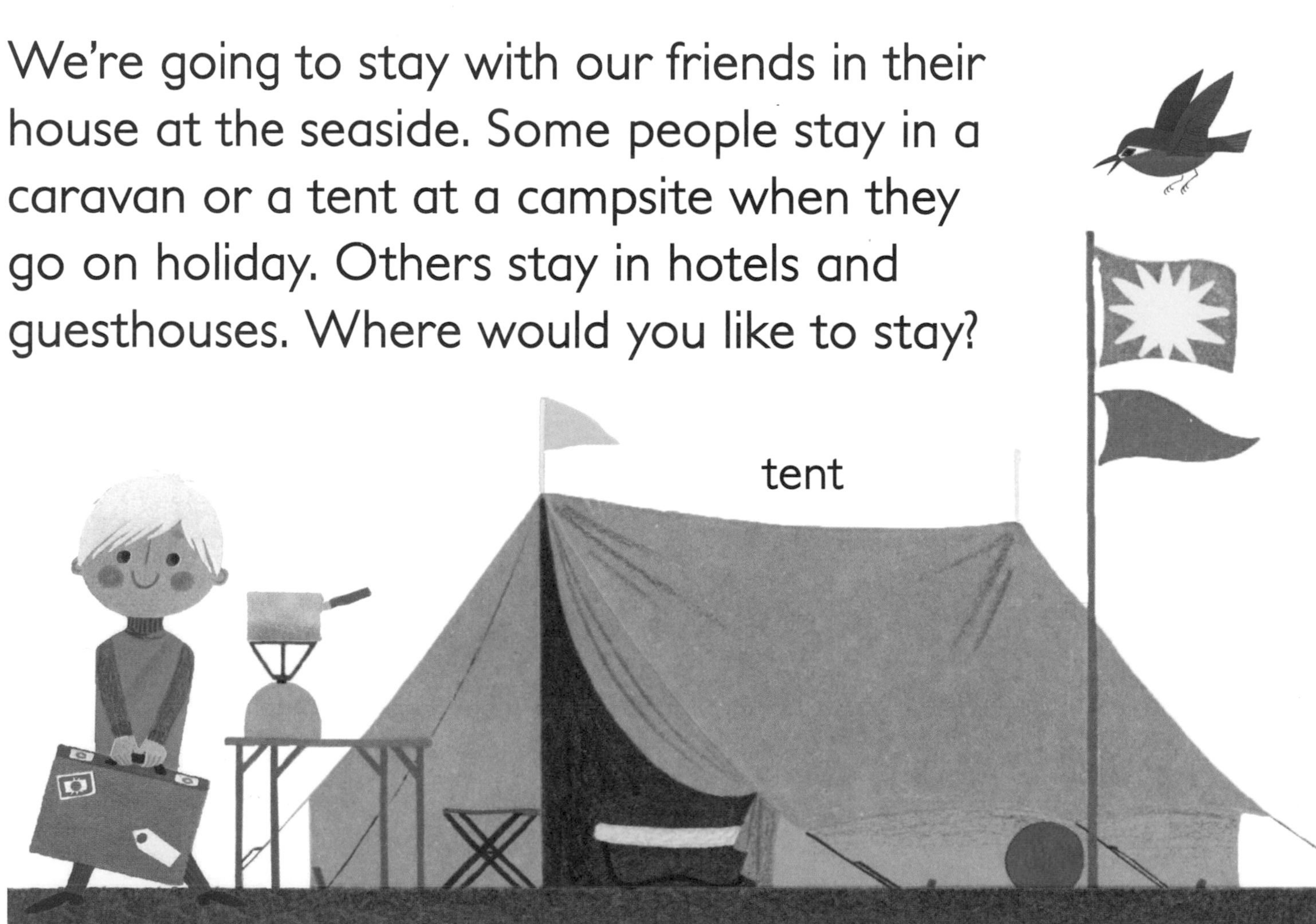

After a long journey on the train we've arrived at our friends' house by the sea. We go to bed and dream about going to the beach tomorrow. What will it be like, we wonder?

27
5
95

Fun on the beach

It's our first day at the seaside. There are so many wonderful new things to see. There are boats and a lighthouse.

boat

lighthouse

I'm going to put everything
I can see in my painting of the
beach. Why don't you draw
a picture of the seaside too?

Lots of children are having fun playing on the beach. What shall we do first?

build a sandcastle

paddle in the sea

watch a puppet show

fly a kite

These children are playing volleyball – let's join in!

Sea life

If you look carefully in a rock pool, you can see small creatures. We're going to try to catch them with a fishing net. Don't worry, we'll put them back afterwards.

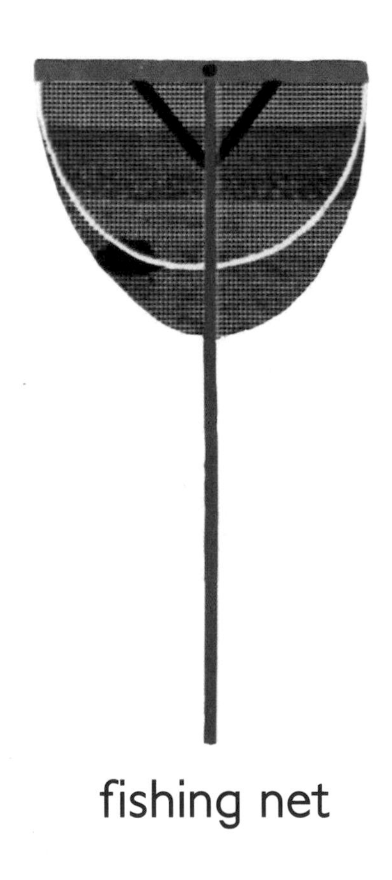

fishing net

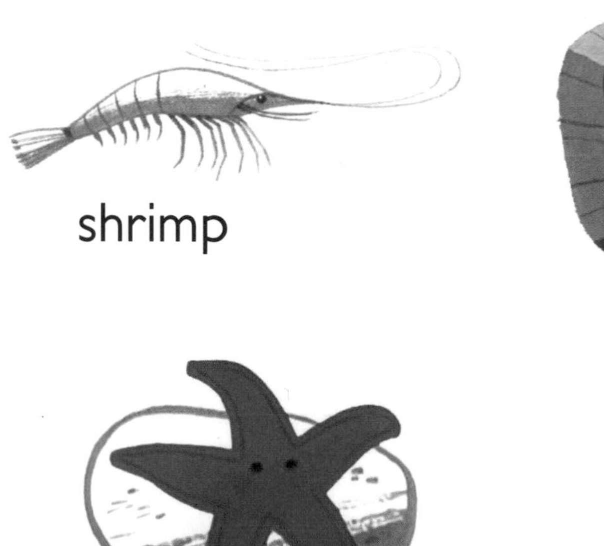

shrimp

barnacle

starfish

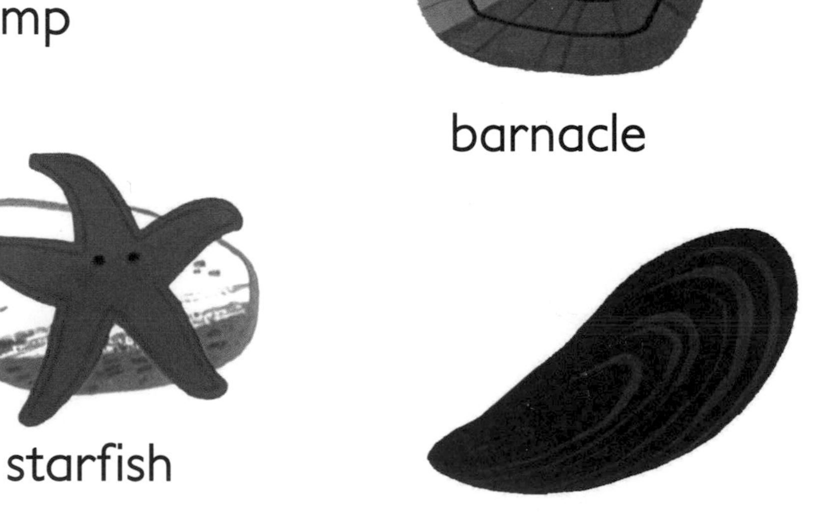

mussel

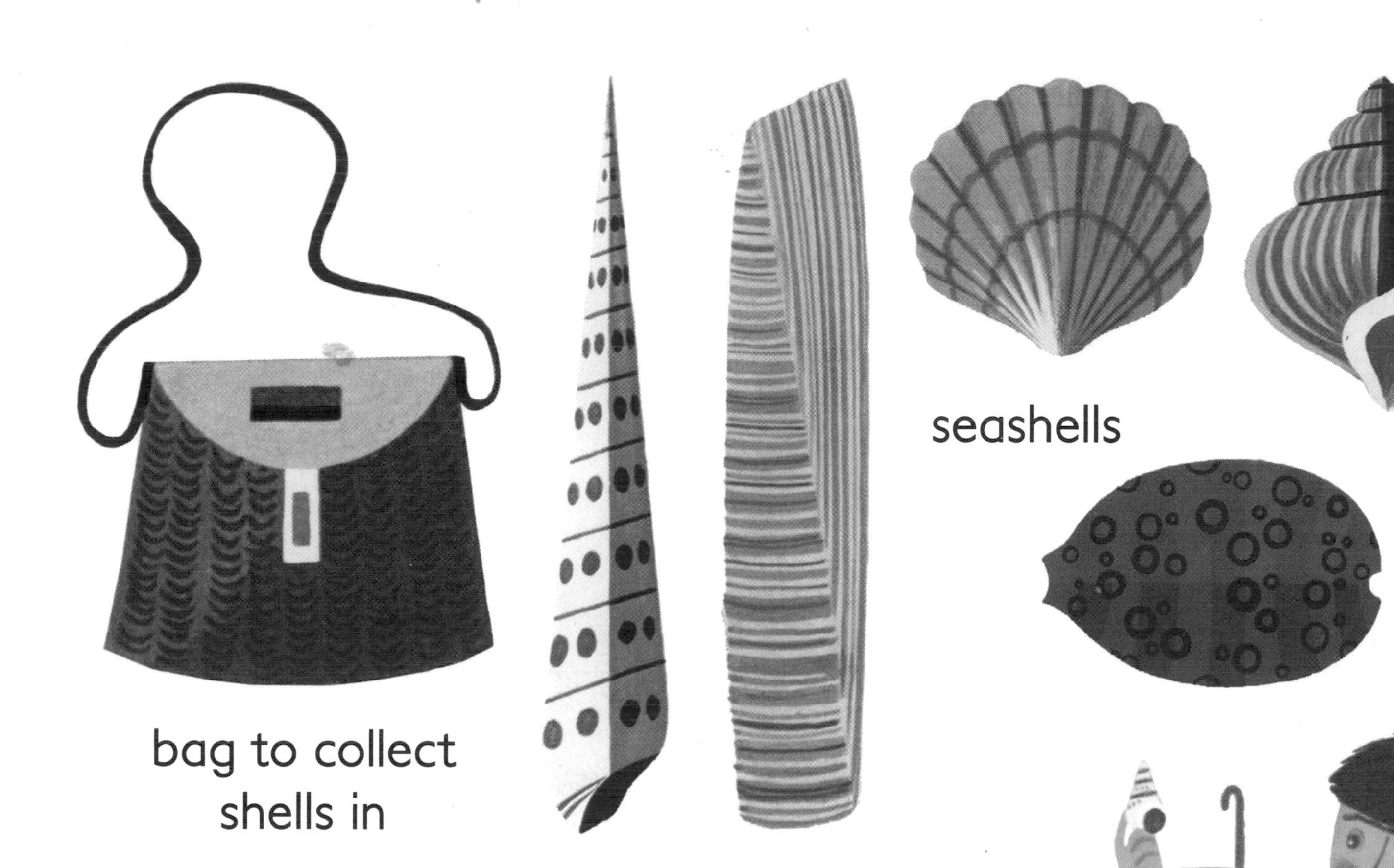

Seashells were once the homes of little sea creatures. They come in many shapes and sizes. Can you copy the shell shapes on this page?

Sea birds

Around the world, many different birds are found at the seaside. Have you seen any of these birds?

pig

black-headed gull

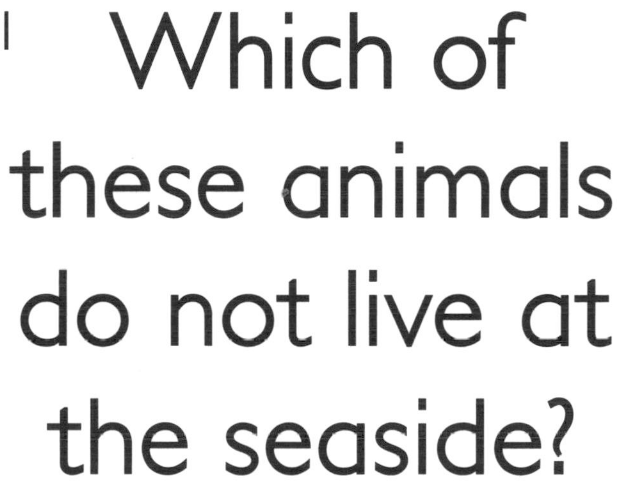

Which of these animals do not live at the seaside?

lobster

lion

hermit crab

octopus

bear

Picnic time

We're having a picnic lunch on the beach. What would you choose to eat?

Food tastes even more delicious when you eat outdoors.

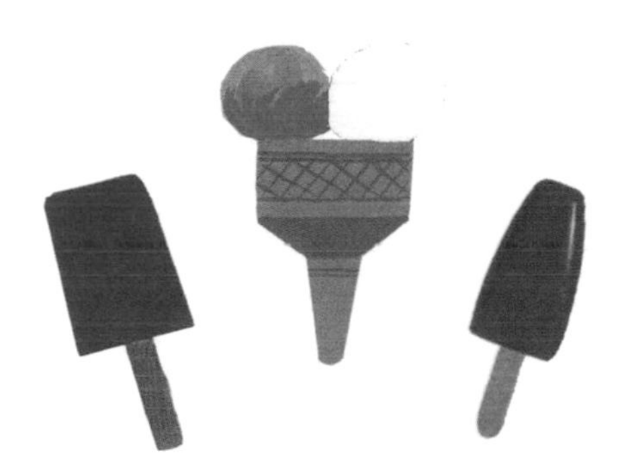

After lunch, we can have an ice cream as a special treat. We buy our ice creams from a lady on the beach.

On the water

Look at all the people having fun on the water. Have you ever seen people windsurfing or waterskiing?

windsurfer

Which of these different kinds of boat can you see in the picture opposite?

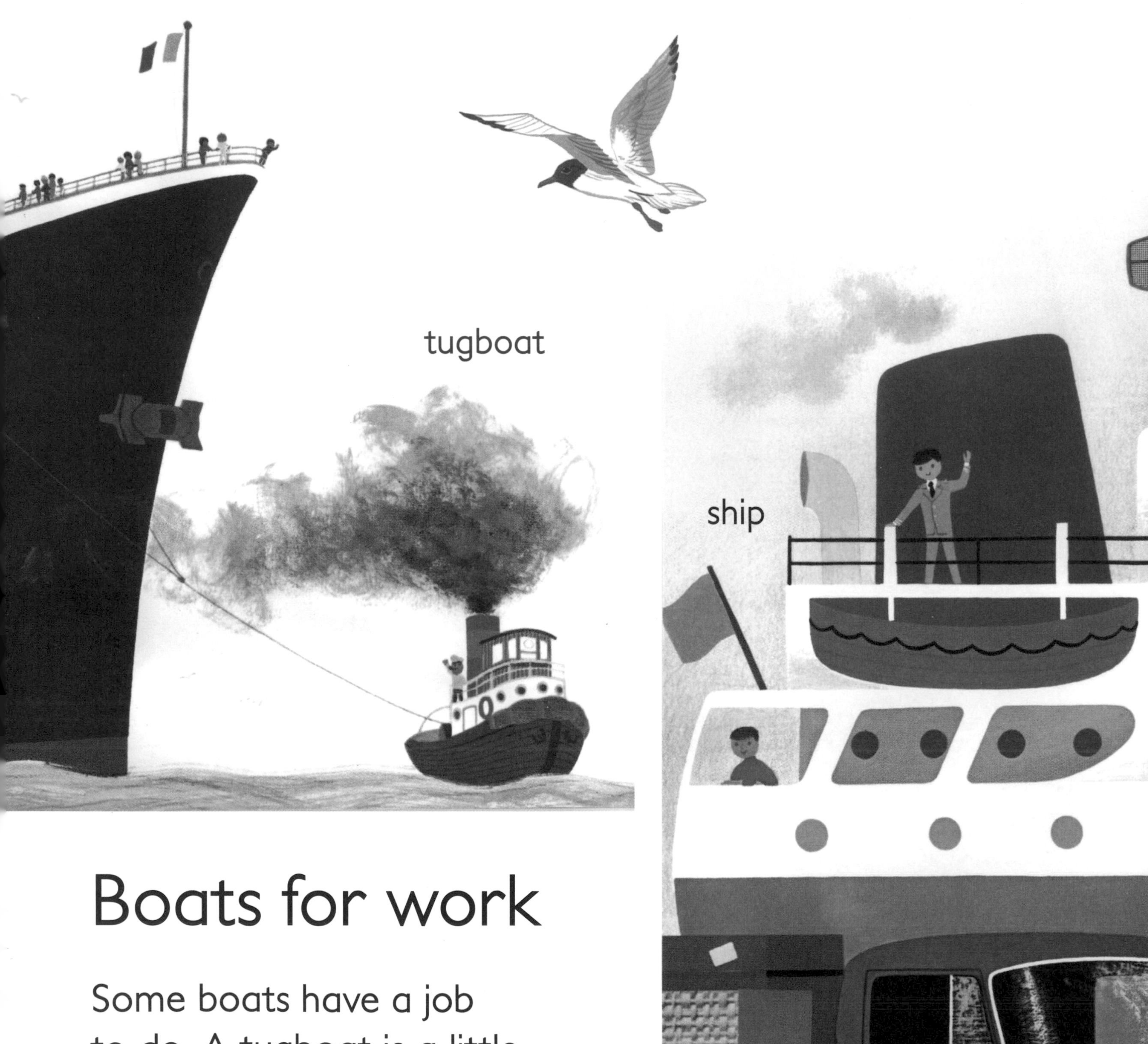

Boats for work

Some boats have a job to do. A tugboat is a little boat that guides large boats safely into the port.

Large ships arrive at the port. Workers unload the cargo – big boxes full of goods for us to buy. They load up the empty ships with goods to carry to countries far away.

Fishing at sea

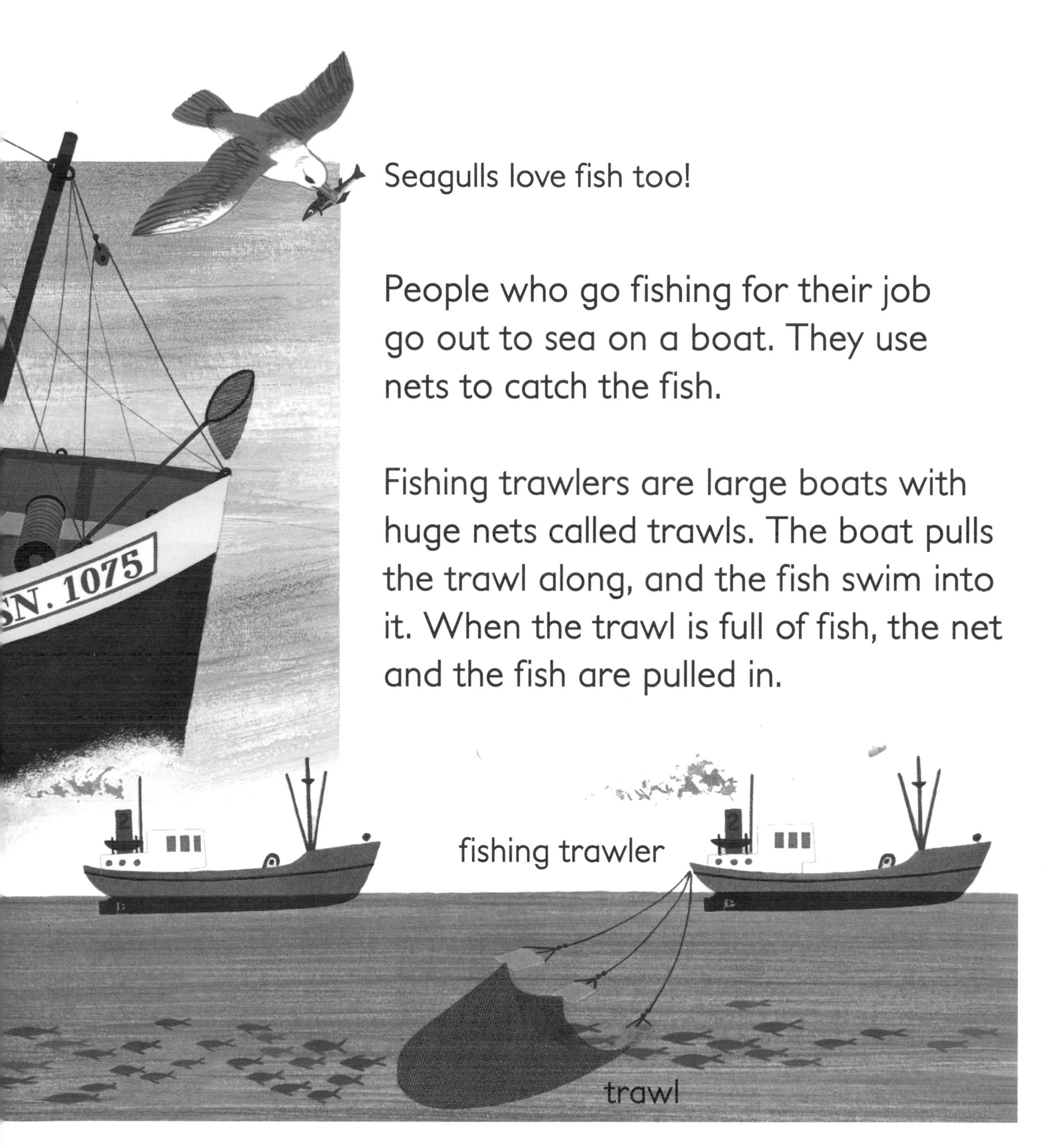

Seagulls love fish too!

People who go fishing for their job go out to sea on a boat. They use nets to catch the fish.

Fishing trawlers are large boats with huge nets called trawls. The boat pulls the trawl along, and the fish swim into it. When the trawl is full of fish, the net and the fish are pulled in.

Fish and shellfish

Fishing boats bring in fish and shellfish for people to eat. What's the difference? Shellfish have a shell! Which creatures below are fish and which are shellfish?

Which of these animals do you think can swim?

Under the sea

With a mask and snorkel you can swim under water.

To go deeper down in the sea, divers need a special outfit and oxygen tanks. Can you match the equipment to the diver on the page opposite?

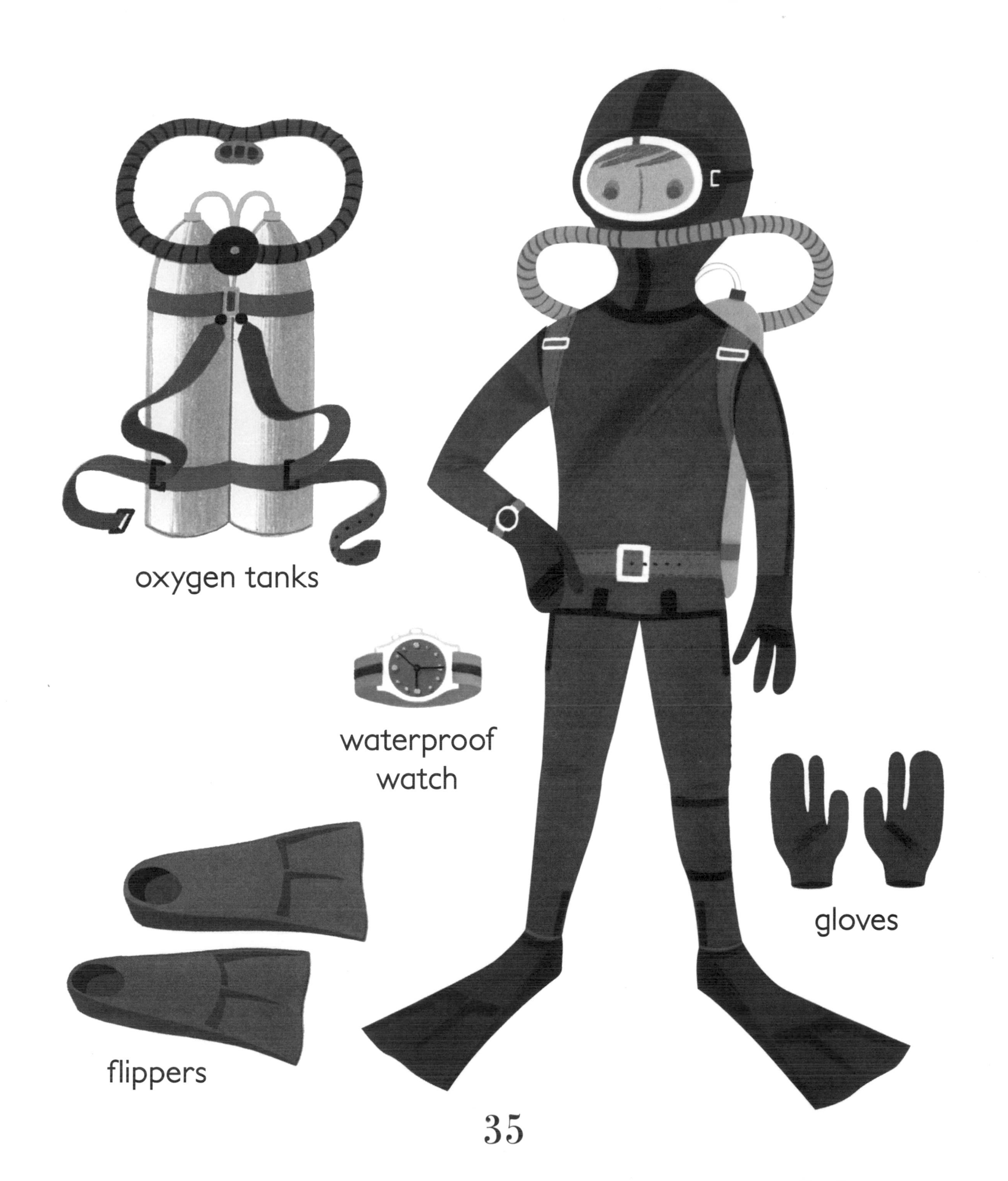
oxygen tanks
waterproof watch
gloves
flippers

Now we're all set to do some snorkelling and diving under the water. What will we find there?

Lots of amazing plants and animals live under the water. You can see colourful starfish, coral, sponges and seaweed when you go diving or snorkelling.

In a submersible, you can go down very deep in the water to see the plants and animals that make their homes on the seabed.

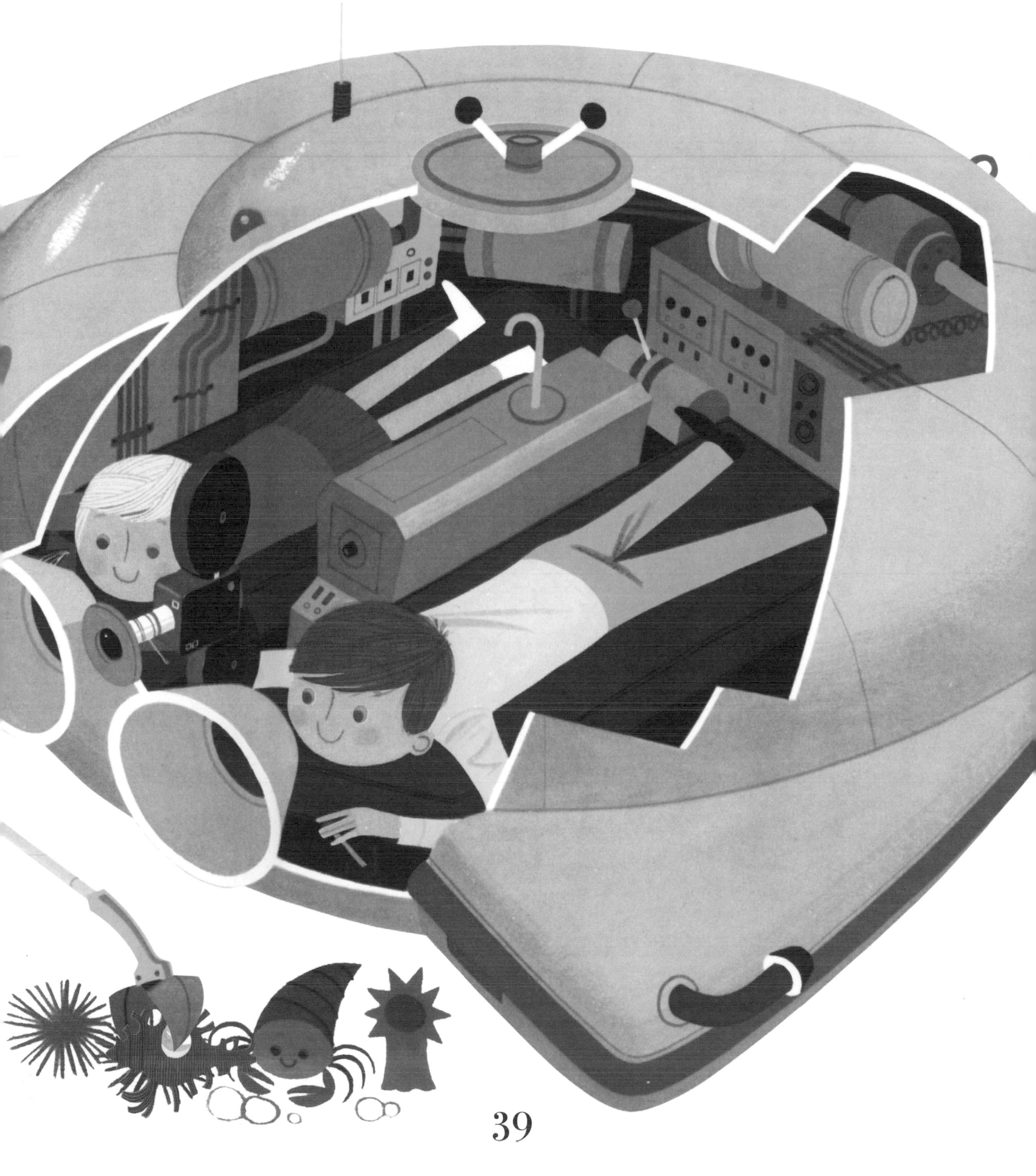

Seaside safety

The seaside is a fun place to be but you need to take care. Here are some tips to keep you and the wildlife safe.

Never throw a glass bottle into the sea. If it breaks, it can hurt people or wildlife.

Always put starfish back in the sea so they don't die.

If you see a bird's nest, look but never touch. You mustn't disturb the birds.

Please don't bury rubbish in the sand. Pop it in a bin or take it home with you.

Always paddle or swim with a grown-up nearby.

Never pour chemicals into the sea. They can poison birds and animals.

When it's hot, wear a sunhat and suncream. Remember to drink lots of water.

Always put sea creatures back where you found them.

Leave large stones on the beach. Sea creatures live under them.

When it's dark, light from the lighthouse warns boats not to crash into rocks.

Spot the difference

Some things have changed in the picture below.
Can you spot eight differences?

ALAIN GRÉE

For more on Button Books, contact:

GMC Publications Ltd
Castle Place, 166 High Street, Lewes, East Sussex, BN7 1XU
United Kingdom
Tel +44 (0)1273 488005
www.gmcbooks.com